The **ABCs** of Keyboarding

A typing manual for beginners

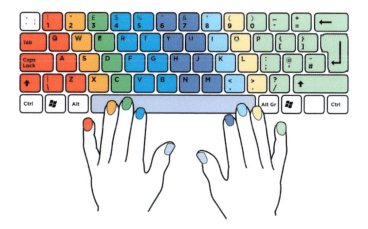

D. Tillson

CONTENTS

ACKNOWLEDGEMENTS

My sincere thanks for the support of all my children, with special thanks to my son, Dwight, who for the last six years has encouraged and supported me in putting together these typing manuals; and to Mr. Les Rivera, Professor of ESL at Clark College, Vancouver, WA.

Also, my appreciation to my long-time and dear friend, K. Juvet, who made the final draft possible.

PREFACE

This manual was inspired by the many English-as-a-Second-Language students who are not only learning a new language and a new alphabet, but also how to type on a computer.

INTRODUCTION

WELCOME NEW TYPIST!

This can be a smooth introduction to the English alphabet plus it will help to make your typing easier and more expedient.

The English Alphabet:

Aa	Jj	Ss
Bb	Kk	Tt
Cc	Ll	Uu
Dd	Mm	Vv
Ee	Nn	Ww
Ff	Oo	Xx
Gg	Pp	Yy
Hh	Qq	Zz
Ii	Rr	

It is best to break your lessons into several study periods so you can add more letters as you progress. A suggested study plan would be to begin lesson 1 and 2 on your first day and practice for about an hour for the next couple days; and then move on to lesson 3, and practice for about an hour and then move on to the remaining lessons, practicing after each lesson.

If you are using a laptop, it would be good to disable the touchpad so you won't lean on the touchpad and get off track. Also, you will then be able to rest your wrists to be able to be more accurate.

Some laptops don't have dedicated buttons but you can use Function keys (like Fn + F5 on Dell computers) to toggle the state of your touch pad.   In the case of HP laptops, you can hold the top-left corner of the touchpad for a few seconds and it will disable the touch pad – repeat this to re-activate it.

New laptop computers either have a physical on/off button to easily disable the touch pad or there's an icon in the system tray that lets you manage the various settings of the touchpad. If you don't have that icon, you can go to Control Panel – > Mouse Properties – > Touch Pad   to enable or disable the touchpad.

I hope you enjoy this typing experience.

NOTES

LESSON 1

The Home Keys, the Enter Key and the Space Bar

The middle row of letters on a keyboard is the home row. The **HOME KEYS** are **A S D F and J K L ;** They are known as the **HOME KEYS** because this is where your 8 fingers rest when not typing. Most keyboards have small bumps on the **f** and **j** keys to help you find the home row without looking at the keys. Find the small bumps on your keyboard.

Position your right hand so that your index finger is placed on **j**, your middle finger is on **k**, your ring finger is on **l** and your pinky (little finger) is on **;** (the semicolon key). Let your right thumb rest comfortably on the spacebar at the bottom of the keyboard.

Position your left hand so that your index finger is on **f**, your middle finger is on **d**, your ring finger is on **s** and your pinky is on **a**. Your thumb can rest on the spacebar.

Now practice placing your fingers on the home keys without looking.

Use the ENTER key to end a paragraph and start a new one. Pressing ENTER twice puts a line of blank space between lines of text.

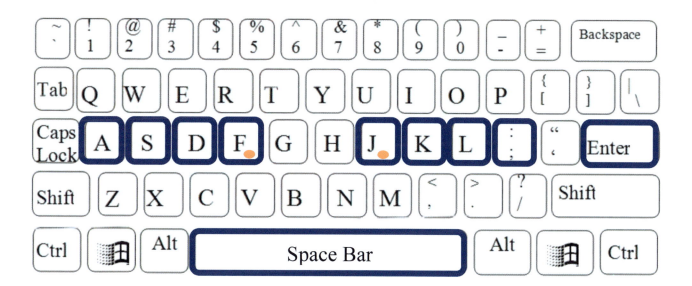

The SPACE BAR puts a space between characters or words.

Practice using the space bar. Space once (tap the space bar once), then twice, then once, then twice. Repeat.

LESSON 2

Left-Hand Letters: **A, B, C, D, E, F, G**

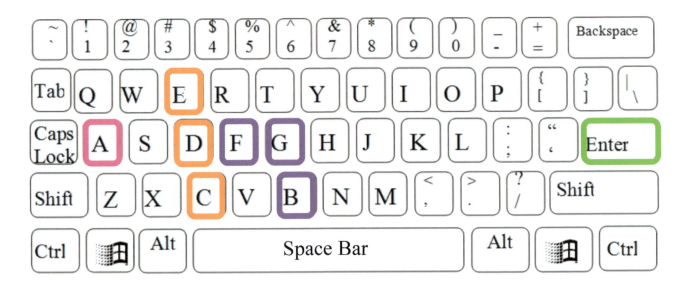

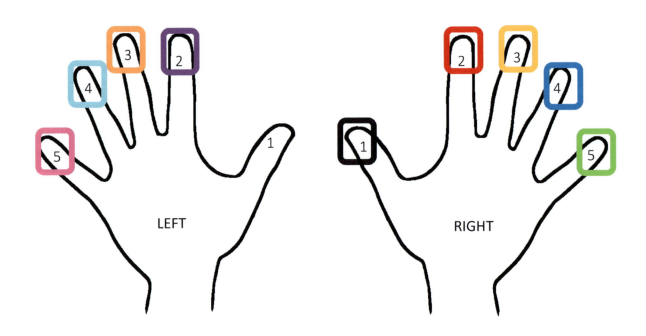

LEFT   RIGHT

LESSON 2

Left-Hand Letters: A, B, C, D, E, F, G — Practice

Type the first practice word and then press ENTER to go to the next line. Continue typing the practice words.

ace

add

age

bad

be

bed

beg

big

cab

dad

dead

deaf

edge

fad

fed

feed

gab

Notes

LESSON 3

Right-Hand Letters: **H, I, J, K, L, M, N, O, P**

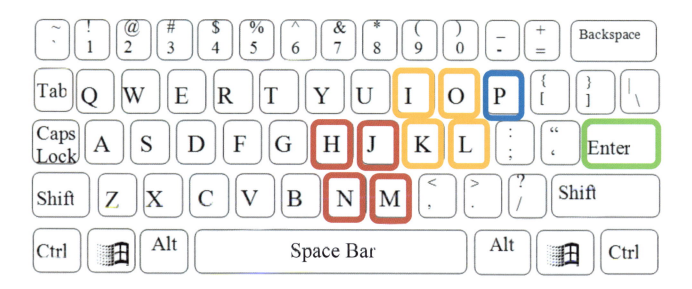

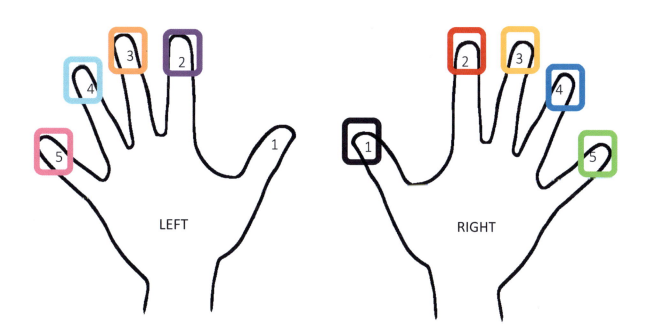

LESSON 3

Right Hand Letters: **H, I, J, K, L, M, N, O, P** — Practice

Type the first practice word and then press ENTER to go to the next line. Continue typing the practice words.

hop

ill

inn

jill

lip

look

loop

milk

monk

mop

no

nip

oil

pill

pin

plop

pop

LESSON 4

Left-Hand Letters: **Q, R, S, T**

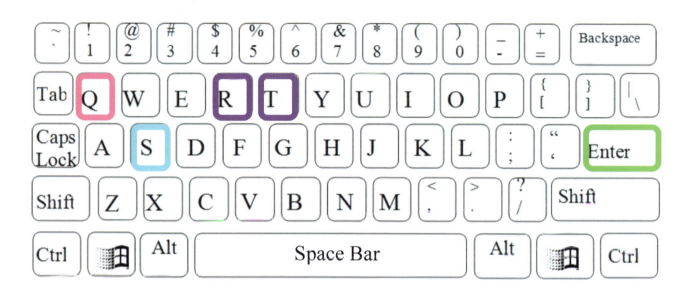

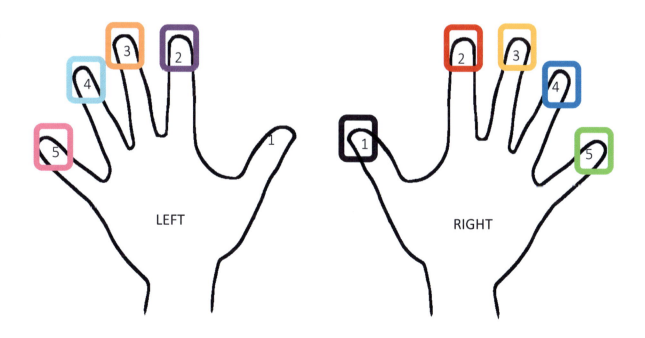

LEFT   RIGHT

LESSON 4

Left-Hand Letters: Q, R, S, T — Practice

Type the first practice word and then press ENTER to go to the next line. Continue typing the practice words.

race

radar

raft

rat

rear

rest

sat

see

seed

set

tar

tea

teeter

test

Notes

LESSON 5

Left- and Right-Hand Letters: **U, V, W**

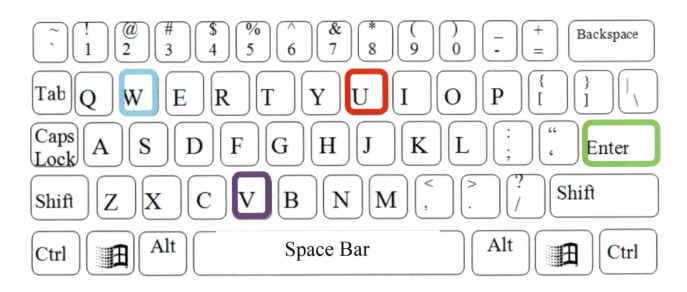

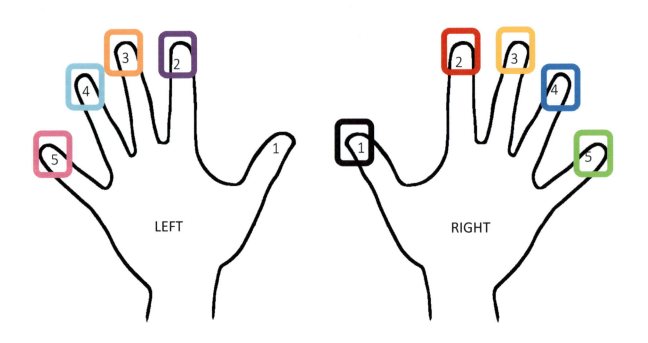

LEFT   RIGHT

LESSON 5

Left- and Right-Hand Letters: **U, V, W** — Practice
Type the first practice word and then press ENTER to go to the next line. Continue typing the practice words.

applaud	umbrella
bundle	understand
conduct	until
daughter	urgent
envelope	use
equal	vest
fortune	victor
glue	violent
hour	violet
how	voice
injure	volunteer
jump	walker
knuckle	westward
natural	who which what where when
television	winter
towel	worker

The ABCs of Keyboarding

LESSON 6

Left- and Right-Hand Letters: **X, Y, Z**

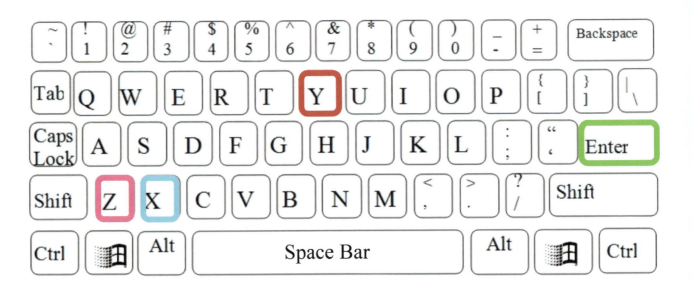

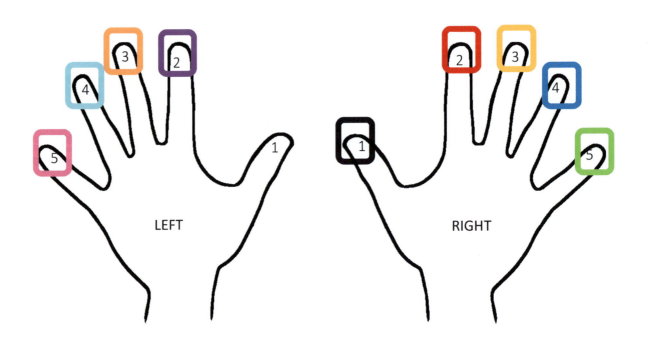

LEFT   RIGHT

LESSON 6

Left- and Right-Hand Letters: **X, Y, Z** — Practice

Type the first practice word and then press ENTER to go to the next line. Continue typing the practice words.

maybe

trinity

xenon

year

xylophone

yacht

yahoo

yank

yard

yarn

yeast

zanadu

zany

zerox

zilch

zipper

zodiac

zombie

zone

Notes

LESSON 7

PRACTICE MAKES PERFECT!

NOW, REPEAT ALL PRACTICES ON <u>PAGES 13, 15, 17, 19 AND 21.</u>

THEN PROCEED TO ADDITIONAL PRACTICES IN THIS LESSON 7.

LESSON 7

All Left-Hand Letters – **A B C D E F G and Q R S T V W X Z** — Practice

Type the first practice word and then press ENTER to go to the next line. Continue typing the practice words.

after

beaver

cards

dear

ever

fast

get

reset

save

stab

tears

vest

wade

zebra

LESSON 7

All Right-Hand Letters: **H I J K L M N O P and Y** — Practice

Type the first practice word and then press ENTER to go to the next line. Continue typing the practice words.

hiho

hip

hop

ill

in

jill

john

kill

kiln

kin

loop

lop

milk

mill

monk

no

oily

pill

poppy

up

yip

LESSON 7

Right and Left Hands - **All letters A through Z** — Practice

Type the first practice word and then press ENTER to go to the next line. Continue typing the practice words.

aqua	ladle
auction	magic
avoid	marvel
bench	neutron
beyond	noble
chance	opera
cheat	orchid
distance	pelican
divide	percent
evening	quail
example	retire
finger	retreat
finish	servant
golden	shadow
goulash	stale
hurry	tar
hygiene	test
interview	udder
jewel	vacant
judge	warm
knot	xylograph
know	yoga
labor	zero

LESSON 7

Right- and Left-Hand Letters: **Q, U** — Practice

Type the first practice word and then press ENTER to go to the next line. Continue typing the practice words.

antique

equation

quack

quadrant

quake

quarantine

quarrel

quart

quarter

quartet

queen

question

queue

quiche

quick

quiet

quilt

quit

quite

quota

quotation

quote

Notes

LESSON 8

The use of the SHIFT Key

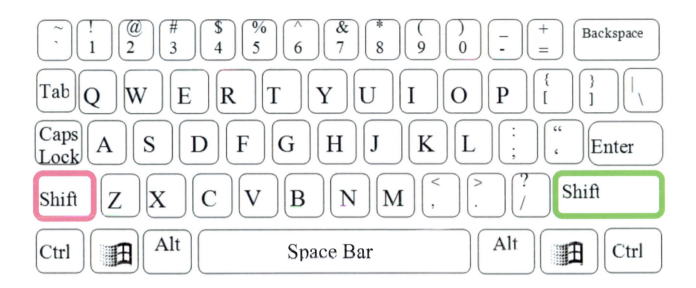

The main use of the SHIFT key is to move from lower case (small letters) to upper case capitals (big letters). By pressing the SHIFT key with the letter, you create a capital letter. Capital letters are used when writing proper names or titles and to begin a sentence. It is best to use this key rather than the caps lock as the caps lock makes the letters stay capitalized until pressed again. Sometimes we forget to press it again and then our words are all caps! Since there are 2 shift keys, the left hand will use the left shift key (5th finger) and the right hand will use the right shift key (5th finger).

The other use of the shift key is to activate the symbol on the upper half of the keys.
Example: the slash key also becomes the question mark.

Here are other examples of these keys:

- Semi-colon (;) becomes colon when shift key is added (:)
- Hyphen (-) becomes an under score (_)
- Apostrophe (') becomes a quotation mark (")

Look at your keys; you will see many other keys that change when the shift key is added

> Creates a new **Line Break**
 (↵) or what is referred to as a **Soft Return**. Not a paragraph break.

Notes

LESSON 9

Comma, Period, Forward Slash, Question Mark

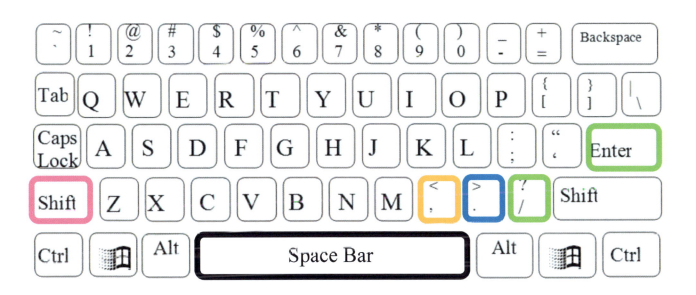

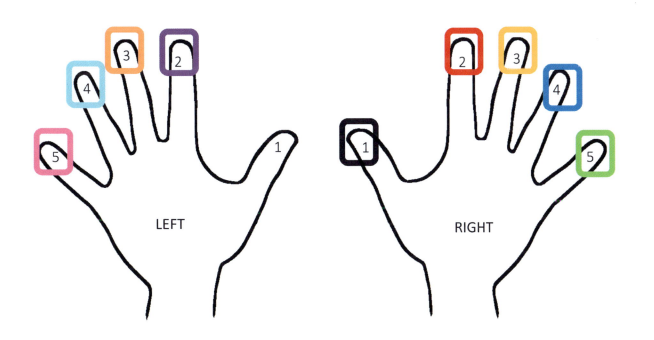

LEFT   RIGHT

LESSON 9

Comma, Period, Forward Slash, Question Mark — Practice
Use the SHIFT Key to type capital letters and the question mark (?) Use the SPACE BAR to put a space between the words. Press the ENTER key twice to get a blank space between the sentences.

Do you come to the conversation groups?

Come to the library for free conversation.

There are three libraries that offer conversation groups.

The libraries that are close by are Battle Ground, Cascade Park, and Ridgefield.

Libraries always have flags flown above their buildings.

Did you know that libraries offer more than book lending?

You can also work on computers at any of these libraries.

Magazines can also be checked out at libraries.

The section for children offers books for young readers, as well as activities.

The comma guides actors and readers by giving pause.

Commas also improve the quality of a sentence.

Commas also divide items in lists.

On my way home, I like to stop at the bookstore.

At the same time, I realized it was possible.

LESSON 10

Hyphen and Dash; Underscore; Colon and Semi-colon; Quotation Marks and Apostrophe; Exclamation Mark; Backspace

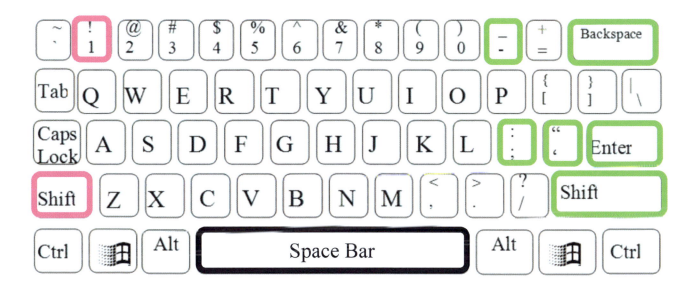

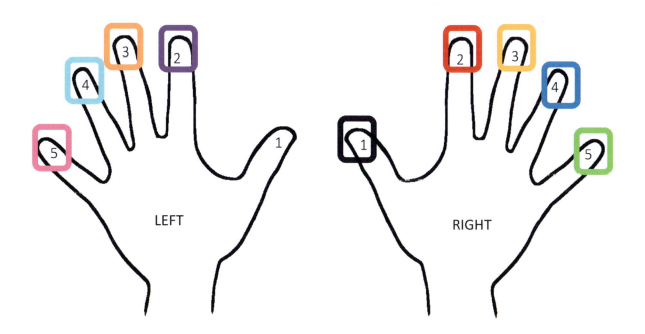

LEFT   RIGHT

LESSON 10

Hyphen and Dash; Underscore; Colon and Semi-colon; Quotation Marks and Apostrophe; Exclamation Mark; Backspace

The HYPHEN and DASH are different, even though they use the same symbol. The small bar (-) next to the = sign is used for hyphenated words, such as t-shirt and twenty-five. The dash can be used like a comma, to separate a part of a sentence. Use two hyphens to make a dash.

Examples of dash and hyphen:

The typist used two hyphens -- another way to create a dash -- to create her sentence.

Woodrow Wilson said the hyphen was "un-American."

Many words require hyphens to avoid confusion. Words such as:
co-respondent
long-standing
re-formed

The man straightened up -- he realized his back was no longer in pain. (dash)

This mentions punctuation -- and how it is used. (dash)

Underscore:

The UNDERSCORE is made using the SHIFT key with the hyphen. The underscore is commonly used when a space is not allowed, such as when giving a file name and saving that file, example "typing_lesson_1." Or to draw a line _____ by pressing the underscore several times in a row.

Examples of Colon and Semi-colon:

The differences: a comma lists more than one item. The hat she bought was red, blue, and green.

The semi-colon is usually used to join separate items that are closely related. He won the bet; she rode the horse.

The colon is three or more items – usually in a list. I like the following: peas, carrots, and string beans.

Examples of Apostrophe and Quotation Marks:

The apostrophe often fills in dropped letters: it's, (for it is) I'm (for I am), isn't (for is not), and don't (for do not). These are called contractions.

It also shows possession: the boy's hat (the hat belongs to the boy), the girl's shoes, the baby's bib.

The backspace was used very little in the past and not used to correct like currently used. It is now used to delete the text to the left of the cursor.

LESSON 10

Hyphen and Dash; Underscore; Colon and Semi-colon; Quotation Marks and Apostrophe; Exclamation Mark; Backspace — Practice

Use the SHIFT Key to type capital letters and the underscore (_), colon (:), quotation mark ("), question mark (?) and exclamation mark (!). Use the SPACE BAR to put a space between the words. Press the ENTER key twice to get a blank space between the sentences.

Have you ever heard of the "Polar Express?"

"There," said the conductor, "is the North Pole."

"All aboard," the conductor cried out.

"There is no Santa," my friend insisted.

Santa asked, "What would you like for Christmas?"

Wow! The views are wonderful.

On Donner! On Prancer! Called out Santa to the reindeer.

The underscore is used in an email address like this: bill_hamilton@sample.com

I can draw a line using the underscore key by pressing several times _____.

The apostrophe shows the omission of a letter or possession.

Those are Santa's boots by the door.

Do you know all the reindeers' names?

That is your sister's list for Christmas.

All the cards' addresses are correct.

Please save Mom's presents for a surprise.

Don't forget to help the rest of the family.

Isn't that your book of Christmas stories?

I won't be able to sleep because I am so excited!

Where's the party?

I like the following: peas, carrots, and string beans.

You can give Alicia her birthday card -- just make sure to send it on time.

Notes

LESSON 11

PRACTICE MAKES PERFECT!

NOW, REPEAT ALL PRACTICES ON <u>PAGES 29 AND 32</u>.

THEN PROCEED TO ADDITIONAL PRACTICES IN LESSON 13 ON <u>PAGES 35, 36 AND 37</u>.

LESSON 12

Numbers and Symbols

The numbers are located in the top row of the keyboard. The symbols are typed by using the SHIFT key. See the Glossary at the end of this manual for an explanation of these keys.

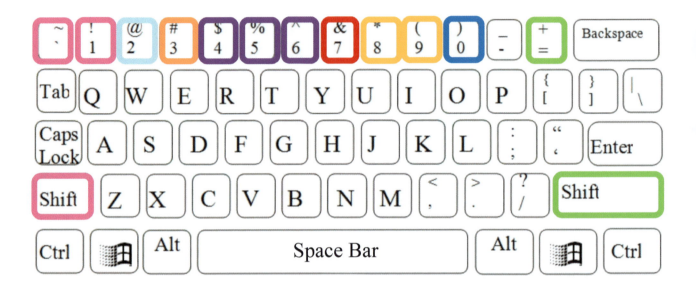

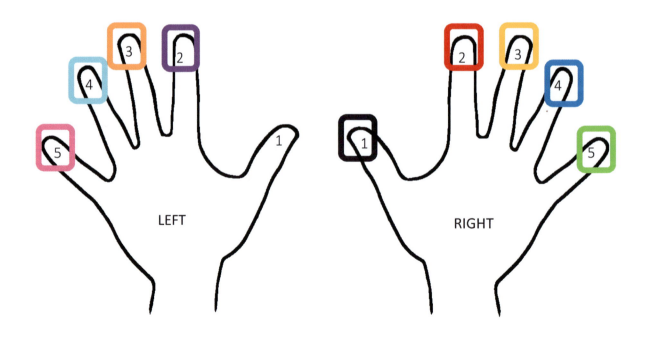

Notes

LESSON 13

PRACTICE MAKES PERFECT!

Sentences

In addition to graduating in the top of my class, I have been a volunteer for a community program.

Stay Awake! Stay Alive! Be well rested. Do not make a long trip without a break.

Avoid driving alone for long distances.

Avoid alcohol and medications that cause drowsiness as a side effect.

Letting your cat spend time outside allows her to be more physically active.

Two roads diverged in the middle of my life, I heard a wise man say.

I took the road less traveled and that has made the difference every night and every day.

He paused to take in the beauty of the world.

Sorry, I was distracted for a moment.

The Columbia River Gorge is worth the trip by itself, with breathtaking views.

The deer are daily visitors and sometimes a serious nuisance.

At last, they enjoyed a few moments of silence.

LESSON 13

PRACTICE MAKES PERFECT!

Paragraphs

We all want the best for our children. We want the best schools, the best doctors, the best foods. But often we give little thought to the environment where our children live, and the quality of the air they breathe. Some of us smoke with our children sitting right next to us. We bring home dinner from a fast food restaurant because it is cheap, or cook leftover lasagna in the microwave because it is convenient. We spray pesticides on the lawns where our children play and set off roach bombs in the rooms where they sleep. We use chlorine bleach, ammonia, and dozens of other toxic chemicals to clean the clothes our children wear, and the plates they eat on, and the carpets they lay on to watch TV.

Stay Awake! Stay Alive! Be well rested. Do not make a long trip without a break. Avoid driving alone for long distances. Avoid alcohol and medications that cause drowsiness as a side effect.

What is birth order--and should anyone care? Absolutely! Your birth order, whether you were born first, second, or later in your family, has a powerful influence on the kind of person you will be, the kind of person you will marry, the type of occupation you will choose -- even the kind of parent you will be. Birth order has nothing to do with astrology, but it definitely affects your personality, who you marry, your children, and also your occupational choice.

One of the things that I find so troubling about growing old in America is that we do not fully appreciate the value of experience. And who is more experienced at living than the elderly? Most of us really do not know anything about anything. But we all learn some things through experience.

LESSON 13

PRACTICE MAKES PERFECT

Fill in the Missing Keys on the Keyboard

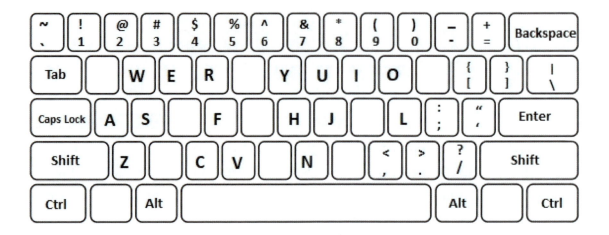

CONGRATULATIONS TYPIST!

You should now be able to find the keys by touch without having to look!

Look at your screen or your master copy (not down at the keyboard) and type away.

You can even practice the alphabet anywhere you are -- as a passenger in the car, or at the lunch table -- just start with the letter A and keep going through the letter Z.

Notes

GLOSSARY

Backspace	Moves the cursor to the left one space at a time, deleting letters or spaces
Caps Lock	Used to type all capital letters until released (pressed again)
Home Row	Where hands are positioned to begin typing, Left fingers are on the a,s,d,and f keys and right fingers are on j,k,l,and ; keys
Return/Enter	Used to enter information into a computer or to return the cursor to the beginning of a new line
Shift	Used to capitalize letters when pressed with that letter key
Space Bar	Spaces the cursor forward one space at a time and produces a blank space when pressed
Tab	Used to move the cursor directly to a tab stop
Apostrophe '	Also known as single quote, indicates the omission of one or more letters, or to indicate a quote within a quote or show possession
@ Sign	The @ sign means each (or ea.), at or each at, as in "Three magazines @ five dollars" (3 magazines would cost $5 each or $15 total). The @ sign is also now a required part of all internet email addresses, for example joe@gmail.com
Tilde ~	An accent (~) placed over Spanish n when pronounced ny (as in señor), or the tilde symbol as a part of a URL (Uniform Resource Locator), or web address
Exclamation Mark !	A punctuation mark used in English and other languages shows a statement of excitement such as extreme happiness, shouting, or surprise. For example: Wow! Unbelievable! That's great! Stop jumping on the bed this instant!
Number Sign #	The pound sign (not to be confused with the Pound symbol showing currency) or hash in various countries. On a phone keypad, it is known as the pound key (U.S.) or hash key in most English-speaking countries.
Dollar Sign $	This symbol represents currency in the US and some other countries and is also used in computer programming
Percent Sign %	The percent sign (%) is the symbol used to indicate a percentage, a number or ratio as a fraction of 100.
Ampersand &	A symbol used to represent the word "and"
Asterisk/Star *	A star-like symbol (*) used in literature, math, computing, and many other fields
Left/Right Parentheses ( )	Used in writing to show an explanation
Left/Right Curly Brackets { }	Unless you are a physicist or a highly skilled mathematician, you are unlikely to encounter curly brackets in your research or reading. If you're a programmer, you would most assuredly use these bygone little squiggly marks.

Left/Right Square Brackets [ ]	Use square brackets when you are inserting material into sentences that are not originally in the sentence--in other words, not done by the original author.
Angle Brackets < >	Angle brackets are used frequently in comic books to show someone speaking in another language. They are also used to show greater than > or less than < in math.
Pipe |	The vertical bar (|) is a computer character with various uses in mathematics, computing, and typography.
Colon/Semi-colon : ;	A punctuation mark consisting of two equally sized dots centered on the same vertical line. A colon is used to explain or start a list. A colon is also used with ratios; titles and subtitles of books; city and publisher in bibliographies; business letter salutation; hours and minutes; and formal letters. The semicolon or semi-colon is a punctuation mark that separates major sentence elements. A semicolon can be used between two closely related independent clauses. Semicolons can also be used in place of commas to separate items in a list, particularly when the elements of that list contain commas.
Hyphen -	A short punctuation mark used to join words (such as well-read or jack-of-all-trades) and to separate syllables of a single word or the characters in a telephone number (123-555-0123).
Dash --	It's not a hyphen; a dash is a short line that serves as a punctuation mark and often represented by one or more hyphens.
Underscore (_)	The underscore is commonly used as an alternative to the space key when a space is not allowed, or when typed repeatedly, a line.
Plus/Equals + =	The plus symbol is used to denote the operation of addition and to indicate that a number is positive. The equals symbol is used in a mathematical expression to indicate the sum of the parts, for example 2 + 3 = 5.
Quotation Marks "	A pair of symbols used at the beginning and end of text that is quoted word for word, dialogue (such as in a book), and around the titles of some short works.
Slash Marks \ /	Back slash and forward slash. A good way to remember the difference between a backslash and a forward slash is that a backslash leans backwards (\ ), while a forward slash leans forward (/). The backslash is used only for computer coding. The forward slash, often simply referred to as a slash, is a punctuation mark used in English, for example 12/31/18 or "You should bring pencil and/or a pen to class."

Notes

Printed in Great Britain
by Amazon